THE BUCK STOPS HERE

THE PRESIDENTS OF THE UNITED STATES

E PLURIBUS UNUM

UPDATED
EDITION

ALICE PROVENSEN

20TH ANNIVERSARY EDITION

VIKING
An Imprint of Penguin Group (USA) Inc.

FOR NINA AND JOSEF SOMMER

VIKING
Published by Penguin Group
Penguin Young Readers Group, 345 Hudson Street, New York, New York 10014, U.S.A.
Penguin Group (Canada), 90 Eglinton Avenue East, Suite 700, Toronto, Ontario, Canada M4P 2Y3 (a division of Pearson Penguin Canada Inc.)
Penguin Books Ltd, 80 Strand, London WC2R 0RL, England
Penguin Ireland, 25 St Stephen's Green, Dublin 2, Ireland (a division of Penguin Books Ltd)
Penguin Group (Australia), 250 Camberwell Road, Camberwell, Victoria 3124, Australia (a division of Pearson Australia Group Pty Ltd)
Penguin Books India Pvt Ltd, 11 Community Centre, Panchsheel Park, New Delhi – 110 017, India
Penguin Group (NZ), 67 Apollo Drive, Rosedale, North Shore 0632, New Zealand (a division of Pearson New Zealand Ltd.)
Penguin Books (South Africa) (Pty) Ltd, 24 Sturdee Avenue, Rosebank, Johannesburg 2196, South Africa

Penguin Books Ltd, Registered Offices: 80 Strand, London WC2R 0RL, England

First published in 1990 by Harper & Row, Publishers
This edition published by Viking, an imprint of Penguin Young Readers Group, 2010

1 3 5 7 9 10 8 6 4 2

The Library of Congress has cataloged the original edition as follows:

Provensen, Alice.
The buck stops here : the presidents of the United States / by Alice Provensen.
p.   cm.
Summary: Detailed pictures and symbols present both personal and political facts about the Presidents
of the United States and some historical events occurring during their terms.
ISBN 0-06-024786-X.—ISBN 0-06-024787-8 (lib. bdg.)
1. Presidents—United States—History—Pictorial works—Juvenile literature.
2. United States—History—Pictorial works—Juvenile literature.
[1. Presidents—Pictorial works. 2. United States—History—Pictorial works.] I. Title.
E176.1.P977   1990   88-35036
973'022'2—dc19   CIP
AC

This edition ISBN 978-0-670-01252-7

Manufactured in China
Set in Goudy Old Style

INTRODUCTION

MY FIRST RECOLLECTION of a presidential election was the campaign of 1928. Coolidge had declined the nomination; Herbert Hoover was running against Al Smith; I was ten years old. I remember roller-skating over the sidewalks of Chicago at twilight, spinning and whirling, and shouting, "I do not choose to run! I do not choose to run!" and then, echoing in the cold November air, "Hoobie Heever! Hoobie Heever for president!"

My earliest national hero was the flier Charles A. Lindbergh. I thought of him and his airplane (and I included myself) as "we."

Born during one World War, growing up during the Great Depression, and coming of age during another World War, I was left with considerable skepticism about politics. Nevertheless, Franklin D. Roosevelt was another of my early heroes (I hoped he would live forever). However, there were presidents before and after whom I have admired.

☆ ☆ ☆

For more than two hundred years, the presidents of the United States have been loved and hated, praised and poked fun at. As men, they were ambitious, clever, opportunistic, honest, or dissembling. Some were confused and ineffectual—bumbling amateurs. A few have been remarkable statesmen. All risked their reputations and their lives by taking office.

In spite of these men—or because of some of them—the office of the presidency has dignity. It has power. It continues to have a central place in the history of our nation and exerts a strong influence on the nations of the world. No foolish puns, no playful nonsense, no vilification or verbal abuse, no derisive caricatures can detract from the glory of that office.

This is not a history book, although it contains a good deal of information about America's past. Its pictures are designed to help readers make connections between the presidents and the events surrounding them. The rhyme may help in remembering our presidents' names and the order in which they served. Perhaps, too, curiosity about our history will be aroused.

☆ ☆ ☆

I must acknowledge my indebtedness to all those anonymous nineteenth-century artists who followed the campaign trails, who illustrated the broadsheets, and who designed the buttons, banners, and cigar bands that helped to elect our presidents. Thanks, too, are due to my editor, Linda Zuckerman, for her invaluable suggestions and contributions.

Notes on the presidents and explanations of the drawings may be found at the back of the book. In this updated edition of the original book, the events of the administrations of George Bush, Bill Clinton, George W. Bush, and Barack Obama have been added.

Alice Provensen

E PLURIBUS UNUM

GEORGE WASHINGTON

1789–1797

1

THE FIRST THIRTEEN STATES

DELAWARE	PENNSYLVANIA	NEW JERSEY	GEORGIA
CONNECTICUT	MASSACHU SETTS	MARY LAND	
SOUTH CAROLINA	NEW HAMPSHIRE	VIRGINIA	
NEW YORK	NORTH CAROLINA	RHODE ISLAND	

179_ FIRST U.S. CENSUS AUTHORIZE_

FIRST

THOMAS JEFFERSON   JOH_ JAY

SECRETARIES OF STAT_

FIRST

TIMOTHY PICKERING

POSTMASTER GENERAL

FIRST VICE PRESIDENT

JOHN ADAMS

"The most insignificant office that ever the invention of man contrived"

FIRST COPYRIGHT LAWS

FIRST U.S. INVENTION WITH MOMENTOUS ECONOMIC CONSEQUENCES 1793

ELI WHITNEY'S COTTON GIN

FIRST

PRESIDENTIA_ FALSE TEETH

NOVUS ★ ORDO

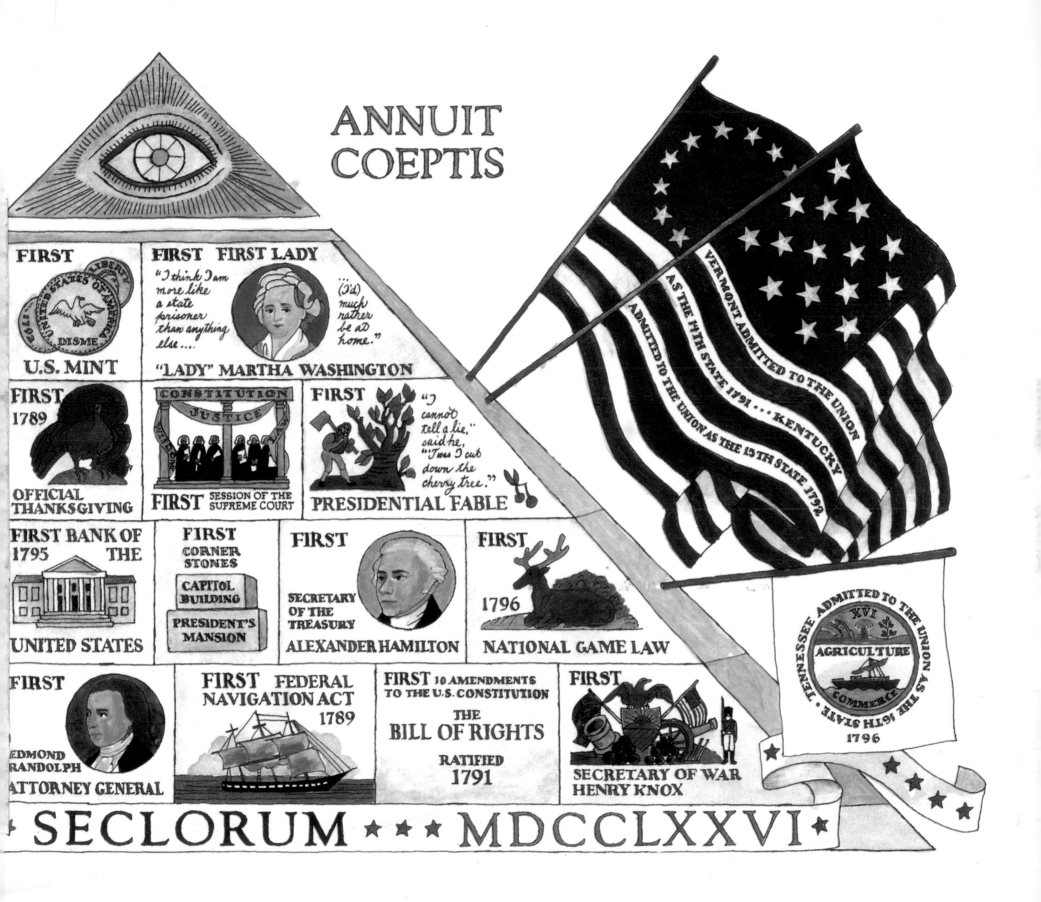

ANNUIT COEPTIS

FIRST
U.S. MINT

FIRST FIRST LADY
"I think I am more like a state prisoner than anything else...."
"...(I'd) much rather be at home."
"LADY" MARTHA WASHINGTON

FIRST 1789
OFFICIAL THANKSGIVING

FIRST SESSION OF THE SUPREME COURT

FIRST
"I cannot tell a lie," said he, "'Twas I cut down the cherry tree."
PRESIDENTIAL FABLE

FIRST BANK OF 1795 THE
UNITED STATES

FIRST CORNER STONES
CAPITOL BUILDING
PRESIDENT'S MANSION

FIRST
SECRETARY OF THE TREASURY
ALEXANDER HAMILTON

FIRST
1796
NATIONAL GAME LAW

FIRST
EDMOND RANDOLPH
ATTORNEY GENERAL

FIRST FEDERAL NAVIGATION ACT 1789

FIRST 10 AMENDMENTS TO THE U.S. CONSTITUTION
THE BILL OF RIGHTS
RATIFIED 1791

FIRST
SECRETARY OF WAR HENRY KNOX

VERMONT ADMITTED TO THE UNION AS THE 14TH STATE 1791 ••• KENTUCKY ADMITTED TO THE UNION AS THE 15TH STATE 1792

TENNESSEE ADMITTED TO THE UNION AS THE 16TH STATE
XVI
AGRICULTURE
COMMERCE
1796

SECLORUM ★★★ MDCCLXXVI

FIRST AND FOREMOST, Washington,
Our best beloved President One.

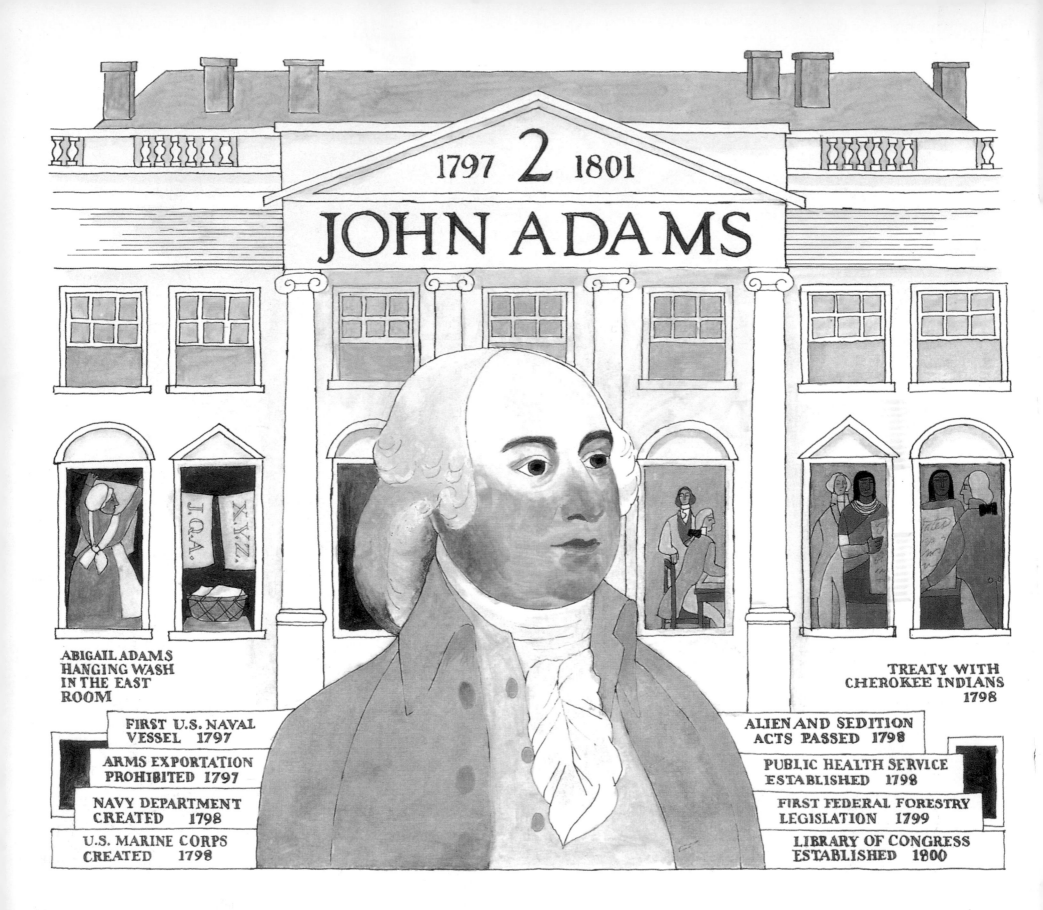

1797 2 1801

JOHN ADAMS

ABIGAIL ADAMS
HANGING WASH
IN THE EAST
ROOM

FIRST U.S. NAVAL
VESSEL 1797

ARMS EXPORTATION
PROHIBITED 1797

NAVY DEPARTMENT
CREATED 1798

U.S. MARINE CORPS
CREATED 1798

TREATY WITH
CHEROKEE INDIANS
1798

ALIEN AND SEDITION
ACTS PASSED 1798

PUBLIC HEALTH SERVICE
ESTABLISHED 1798

FIRST FEDERAL FORESTRY
LEGISLATION 1799

LIBRARY OF CONGRESS
ESTABLISHED 1800

Eloquent Adams, President Two,
Paid court with letters, postage due.

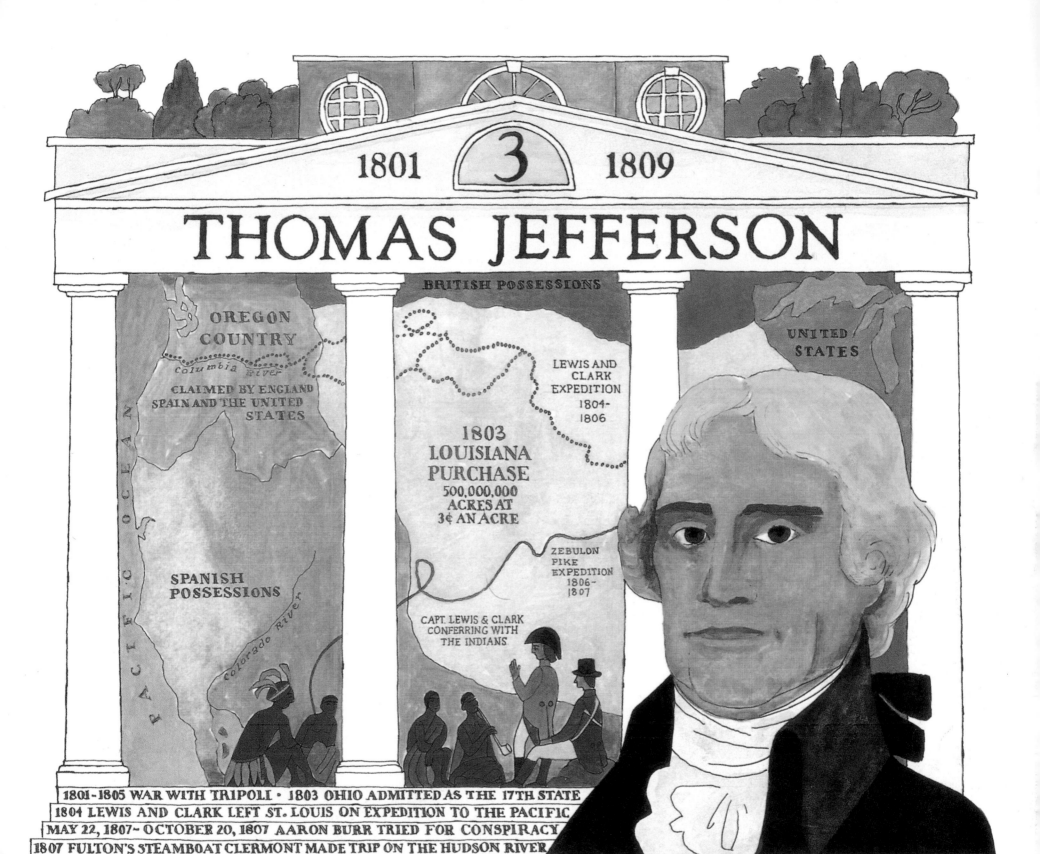

1801 **3** 1809

THOMAS JEFFERSON

BRITISH POSSESSIONS

OREGON COUNTRY

Columbia River

CLAIMED BY ENGLAND SPAIN AND THE UNITED STATES

LEWIS AND CLARK EXPEDITION 1804-1806

UNITED STATES

1803 LOUISIANA PURCHASE 500,000,000 ACRES AT 3¢ AN ACRE

ZEBULON PIKE EXPEDITION 1806-1807

SPANISH POSSESSIONS

Colorado River

CAPT. LEWIS & CLARK CONFERRING WITH THE INDIANS

PACIFIC OCEAN

1801-1805 WAR WITH TRIPOLI · 1803 OHIO ADMITTED AS THE 17TH STATE
1804 LEWIS AND CLARK LEFT ST. LOUIS ON EXPEDITION TO THE PACIFIC
MAY 22, 1807~ OCTOBER 20, 1807 AARON BURR TRIED FOR CONSPIRACY
1807 FULTON'S STEAMBOAT CLERMONT MADE TRIP ON THE HUDSON RIVER

Thomas Jefferson, number Three,
Rigged the Sale of the Century.

VICTORY AT SEA
THE FRIGATE UNITED STATES MET AND DESTROYED
THE H.M.S. MACEDONIAN OCTOBER 25, 1812

DOLLEY MADISON "THE TOAST OF WASHINGTON"
GIVEN A SEAT IN THE HOUSE OF REPRESENTATIVES

THE WAR OF 1812 FOR FREEDOM OF THE SEAS

THE "STAR SPANGLED BANNER" FIRST SUNG 1814

COMMODORE PERRY'S NAVAL VICTORY ON LAKE ERIE 1813

CAPITOL AND WHITE HOUSE BURNED BY BRITISH 1814

DEFEAT OF BRITISH AT NEW ORLEANS 1815

APRIL 30, 1812 LOUISIANA ADMITTED AS 18TH STATE • DECEMBER 11, 1816 INDIANA ADMITTED AS 19TH STATE

Now Madison is number Four.
We're fighting Englishmen once more.

TREATY WITH CHICKASAWS 1818

"GENIUS OF UNIVERSAL EMANCIPATION" ESTABLISHED BY BENJAMIN LUNDY 1820

1817 MISSISSIPPI ADMITTED AS 20TH STATE
1818 ILLINOIS ADMITTED AS 21ST STATE
1819 ALABAMA ADMITTED AS 22ND STATE
1820 MAINE ADMITTED AS 23RD STATE
1821 MISSOURI ADMITTED AS 24TH STATE

THE MISSOURI COMPROMISE 1820

PROHIBITED SLAVERY IN LOUISIANA TERRITORY NORTH OF 36° 30'

THE MONROE DOCTRINE 1823

NO INTERFERENCE IN THE NEW WORLD BY EUROPEAN POWERS

DESIGN OF THE U.S. FLAG ESTABLISHED 1818

FLORIDA ACQUIRED FROM SPAIN 1819

MANUMISSION SOCIETY AND THE QUAKERS • THE EARLY ABOLITIONISTS AND THE UNDERGROUND RAILWAY

Number Five is James Monroe.
He told the world where not to go.

JOHN QUINCY ADAMS

LOUISA ADAMS

1825   1829

ERIE CANAL OPEN

OCTOBER 25, 1825

THE "SECOND JOHN" WAS THE FIRST PRESIDENT WHOSE FATHER HAD ALSO BEEN A PRESIDENT.
"OLD MAN ELOQUENT" WAS THE FIRST PRESIDENT TO WEAR LONG TROUSERS TO HIS INAUGURATION

Remember Adams, number Two?
Well, Six is Adams' son, John Q.

ANDREW JACKSON

THE BANK WARS
1832   1836

"The Bank is trying to kill me but I will kill it!"

TOM THUMB

PETER COOPER'S LOCOMOTIVE

OLD HICKORY · PEOPLE'S PRESIDENT

1829   1837

OSCEOLA · CHIEF OF THE SEMINOLES

REMEMBER THE ALAMO
MARCH 6, 1836

CHESAPEAKE AND DELAWARE

CANAL OPENED
OCTOBER 17, 1829

THE 1833 NEW YORK SUN FIRST DAILY NEWSPAPER

1831·NAT TURNER'S REBELLION~SLAVE UPRISING IN VIRGINIA·1831·ABOLITIONIST W.L. GARRISON PUBLISHES "THE LIBERATOR"
ARKANSAS ADMITTED TO THE UNION AS THE 25TH STATE 1836· MICHIGAN ADMITTED AS THE 26TH STATE 1837

And Seven, seven, Jackson, Andy,
All those coonskins came in handy.

MARTIN VAN BUREN

M. Van Buren, number Eight,
"Ate his meals from a golden plate."

WILLIAM HENRY HARRISON

JOHN TYLER

DIED AFTER ONE MONTH AS PRESIDENT

9 THE AMISTAD DECISION MARCH 9, 1841 — CINQUE — THE ACCUSED AFRICANS OF THE "AMISTAD" REBELLION FREED BY THE SUPREME COURT

PEACE AND TRADE TREATY WITH CHINA · 1844

FIRST MESSAGE OVER MORSE'S TELEGRAPH 1844 "WHAT HATH GOD WROUGHT!" **10** THE CLIPPER "RAINBOW" BUILT FOR THE CHINA TRADE LAUNCHED 1845

Harrison, Nine, went for a ride.
He caught a cold, and so he died.

John Tyler, Ten, tenth President,
Was Head of State by accident.

EXPANSION ~ THE MANIF

TREATY WITH GREAT BRITAIN ESTABLISHING OREGON BOUNDARY · 1846

TEXAS ADMITTED AS 28TH STATE · 1845 ·

JAMES K. POLK

1845 **11** 1849

54°40' OR FIGHT

GOLD DISCOVERED
IN CALIFORNIA
1848

CANADA

— THE FORTY-NINTH PARALLEL —

· 1846 · THE MEXICAN WAR · 1848 ·

MEXICO CEDED TERRITORY THAT BECAME

CALIFORNIA, NEW MEXICO, ARIZONA, NEVADA, UTAH,

AND PARTS OF COLORADO AND

Eleven, eleven, it's Polk we see,
James K. Polk and destiny.

Go west, go west, be brave, be bold!
The land is free, the hills are gold.

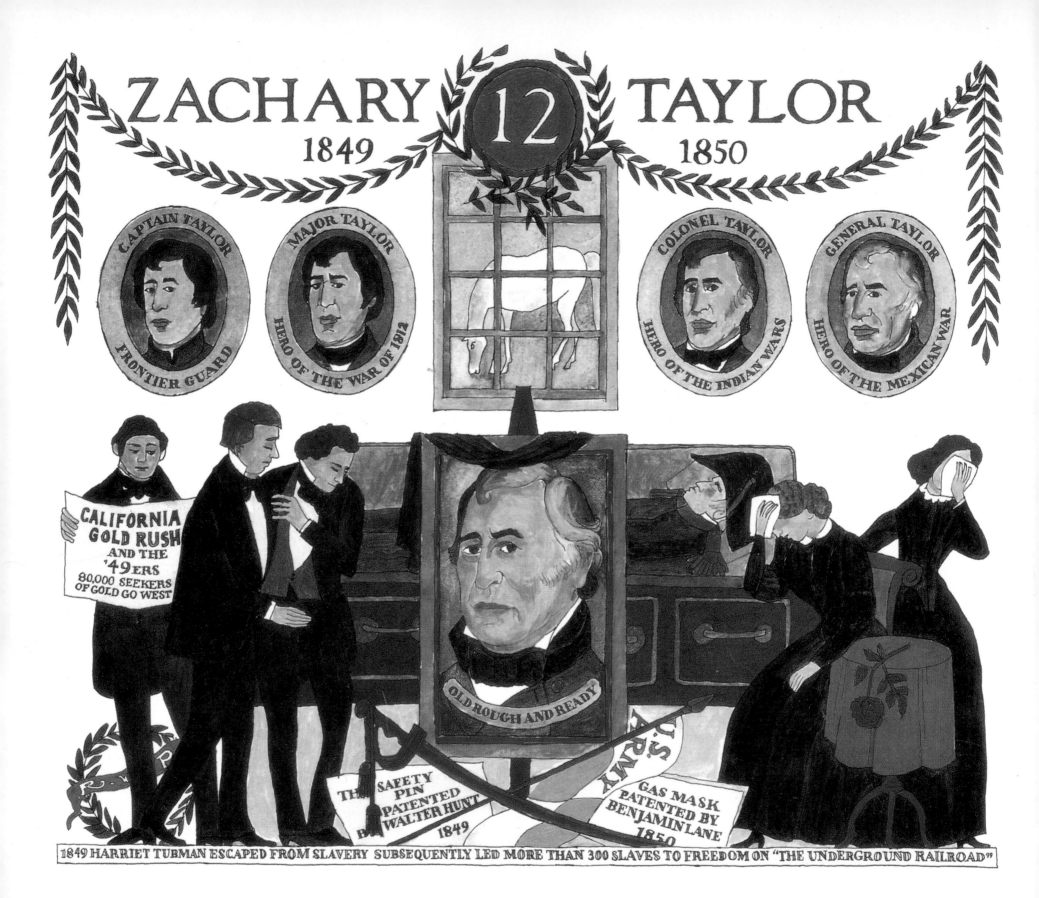

Z. Taylor, Twelve, oh me, oh my.
We thought old soldiers didn't die.

MILLARD **13** FILLMORE
1850 · 1853

CALIFORNIA REPUBLIC

CALIFORNIA ADMITTED TO THE UNION AS THE 31ST STATE 1850

PERRY'S FLAGSHIP

THE MISSISSIPPI

1853 OPENING OF JAPAN TO TRADE BY COMMODORE PERRY

THE COMPROMISE OF 1850

HARRIET BEECHER STOWE

1811-1896

AUTHOR

UNCLE TOM'S CABIN PUBLISHED 1852

1851

FIRST IMPORTED ENGLISH SPARROW SURVIVES IN A CITY PARK

1851 ISAAC SINGER

PATENTED HIS ORIGINAL SEWING MACHINE

MAY 1851
GLEASON'S PICTORIAL

FIRST ILLUSTRATED PICTURE WEEKLY

FIRST CAST-IRON STOVE IN WHITE HOUSE

FIRST WHITE HOUSE BATHTUB WITH RUNNING WATER

Here's lucky Fillmore, Ten and Three—
His hand now turns the White House key.

FRANKLIN PIERCE 1853–1857

Pierce, the Fourteenth White House host,
Ate dinner with a White House ghost.

1857–1861 JAMES BUCHANAN

Fifteen, James Buchanan couldn't
Keep united states that wouldn't.

Oh Sixteen, sixteen, Abraham,
Lincoln was a union man.

Lincoln, Lincoln, Ten and Six,
Betrayed by rogues and lunatics.

Ten and Seven, Johnson, A.
They almost took his job away.

ULYSSES S. GRANT

1869–1877

18

THE GREAT CHICAGO FIRE 1871

THE MYTH OF MRS. O'LEARY'S COW

THE LOWEST EBB 1869

BLACK FRIDAY GOLD SCANDAL

DEPARTMENT OF JUSTICE CREATED 1870

COLORADO ADMITTED TO THE UNION AS THE 38TH STATE 1876

FREDERICK DOUGLASS

EQUAL RIGHTS PARTY

FIRST BLACK VICE-PRESIDENTIAL CANDIDATE 1872

ALEXANDER GRAHAM BELL

FIRST TELEPHONE

1876

NEZ PERCE INDIANS ORDERED TO MOVE TO LAPWAI RESERVATION IDAHO 1877

CHIEF JOSEPH

THE TRANSCONTINENTAL RAILROAD EAST MEETS WEST 1869

PROMONTORY POINT, UTAH

THE DEFEAT OF GENERAL CUSTER

LITTLE BIGHORN 1876

Grant, Eighteen, in general he
Couldn't order the Presidency.

Nineteen, nineteen, strait-laced Hayes,
Sober viewpoint, steadfast gaze.

Garfield, Twenty, in a station,
Departed by assassination.

21 CHESTER A. ARTHUR
1881-1885

THE GREAT EAST RIVER BRIDGE
NEW YORK - BROOKLYN
1883

WASHINGTON
MONUMENT
1885

HOUSE
DECORATION

1882 CHINESE EXCLUSION ACT · 1883 CIVIL SERVICE LAW   1884 LAWS AND FEDERAL COURT PROVIDED FOR ALASKA

Oh, Chester Arthur, Twenty-one,
Deck the halls. Let's have some fun!

GROVER CLEVELAND

BENJAMIN HARRISON

GROVER CLEVELAND

1885-1889

1889-1893

1893-1897

TIPPECANOE

AMERICAN FEDERATION OF LABOR ORGANIZED

INCOME TAX DECLARED UNCONSTITUTIONAL

23

GRANDPA'S GRAND~SON

22

UNCLE JUMBO

1886

1890 SHERMAN ANTI-TRUST ACT

SEPTEMBER 1886 SURRENDER OF THE APACHE GERONIMO PUT AN END TO "FORMAL" WARFARE BETWEEN INDIANS AND WHITES

24

THE PERPETUAL CANDIDATE

1889: NORTH DAKOTA ADMITTED AS 39TH STATE • SOUTH DAKOTA ADMITTED AS 40TH STATE • MONTANA ADMITTED AS 41ST STATE • WASHINGTON ADMITTED AS 42ND STATE • 1890: IDAHO ADMITTED AS 43RD STATE • WYOMING ADMITTED AS 44TH STATE • 1896: UTAH ADMITTED AS 45TH STATE

Grover Cleveland, Twenty-two,
Was honest, good and plenty, too.

Here is Harrison, Twenty-three.
He wears the hat of his granddaddy.

Again it's Cleveland, Twenty-four.
It seems there's always plenty more.

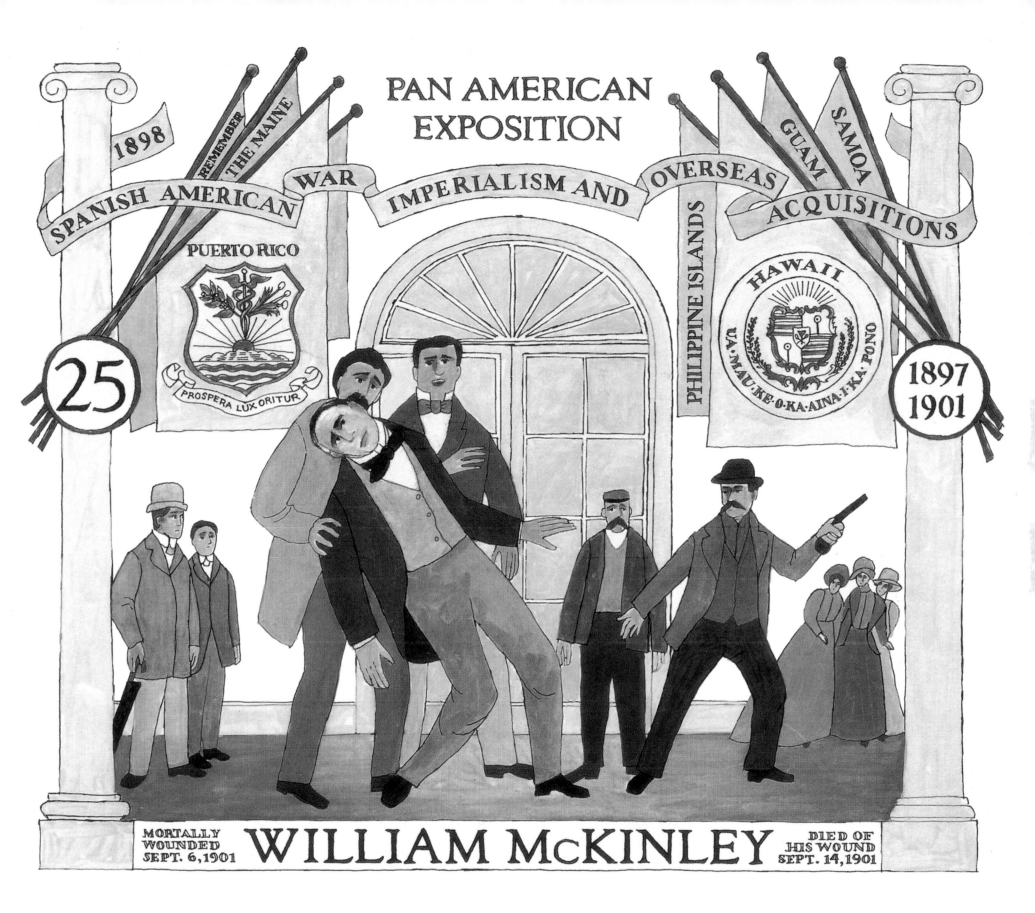

McKinley, Twenty-five, this day
Was shot to death, to his dismay.

26 THEODORE ROOSEVELT

SAN FRANCISCO EARTHQUAKE 1906

THE U.S. RECLAMATION ACT 1902

ELLIS 18

"NO MAN HAS LED A HAPPIER LIFE THAN I HAVE LED... A HAPPIER LIFE IN EVERY WAY."

NOBEL PEACE PRIZE FOR

MEDIATING RUSSO - JAPANESE WAR 1906

1,000,000 IMMIGRANTS A YEAR

1902- ORIENTA A

Teddy Roosevelt, Twenty-six,
Whisper softly, wave big sticks.

1901–1909

THE WRIGHT BROTHERS
FLY THE FIRST POWERED AIRCRAFT
AT KITTY HAWK, N.C. DECEMBER 17, 1903

INVENTION OF THE TEDDY BEAR

ALICE·LEE·ETHEL·QUENTIN·KERMIT·ETHEL·ARCHIBALD

PANAMA CANAL ZONE ACQUIRED 1904

SEEK A NEW LIFE IN AMERICA

MARCONI'S FIRST WIRELESS SIGNAL FROM ENGLAND TO NEWFOUNDLAND 1901

OKLAHOMA 1907 ADMITTED AS THE 46TH STATE

CLUSION 1907 XTENDED

Buy all the land that's way out there.
Go outdoors in your underwear.

WILLIAM HOWARD TAFT

27

1909-
1913

FIRST
U.S. ARMY
AIRPLANE
PURCHASED
AUGUST 2, 1909

CHERRY TREES
PLANTED IN
WASHINGTON

VOTES FOR WOMEN

WOMEN SUFFRAGETTES

ON PARADE 1911

THE WHITE HOUSE ".... is the lonesomest place in the world."

FIRST AUTO KEPT
AT WHITE HOUSE

ADMIRAL PEARY AT
NORTH POLE 1909

NEW MEXICO ADMITTED AS 47TH STATE JANUARY 6, 1912
ARIZONA ADMITTED AS 48TH STATE FEBRUARY 14, 1912

SIXTEENTH AMENDMENT TO THE CONSTITUTION
ESTABLISHES THE INCOME TAX 1913

Here's Twenty-seven, big Bill Taft,
Always graceful, fore and aft.

Thoughtful Wilson, Twenty-eight,
An honest man to celebrate.

WARREN G. HARDING

29

1921-1923

A RETURN TO NORMALCY

BRIBE TAKING

CORRUPTION

LESS GOVERNMENT IN BUSINESS

MORE BUSINESS IN GOVERNMENT

TEAPOT DOME FRAUD

EUGENE V. DEBS PARDONED CHRISTMAS DAY 1921

1921 IMMIGRATION QUOTA LAW ENACTED

ALICE ROBERTSON, FIRST WOMAN TO PRESIDE OVER HOUSE, JUNE 20, 1921
APPOINTED OCT. 3, 1922 : FIRST WOMAN SENATOR, REBECCA L. FELTON

"WHEN MORE AND MORE PEOPLE ARE THROWN OUT OF WORK ... UNEMPLOYMENT RESULTS ..."

1924 ALL UNITED STATES INDIANS GIVEN CITIZENSHIP

TEAPOT DOME SCANDAL INDICTMENTS 1924

THE ROARING TWENTIES AND THE JAZZ AGE

1927 FIRST TALKING MOVIE THE JAZZ SINGER

THE BUSINESS OF AMERICA IS BUSINESS

Harding, Twenty-nine, no doubt
Should have cleaned his Cabinet out.

Silent Thirty,
Coolidge, Cal,

 THE SPIRIT OF ST. LOUIS

AMELIA EARHART'S SOLO FLIGHT ACROSS THE ATLANTIC 1932

CALVIN COOLIDGE
30 1923~1929

HERBERT HOOVER
31 1929~1933

"THE MOMENTUM OF THE ESTABLISHED ORDER REQUIRED THE EXECUTION OF SACCO AND VANZETTI..."

SENTENCED TO DEATH APRIL 27, 1927

12 MILLION UNEMPLOYED

BONUS MARCHERS

APPLES 5¢

BANK CLOSINGS

MORTGAGES FORECLOSED

THE 1929 STOCK MARKET CRASH

THE GREAT DEPRESSION

WHILE PEOPLE MUST NOT SUFFER FROM HUNGER AND COLD, CARING FOR THEM MUST BE PRIMARILY A LOCAL AND VOLUNTARY RESPONSIBILITY

Penny-pincher,
Corporate pal.

Herbert Hoover, Thirty-one,
Is so depressed by what's begun!

FRANKLIN D. ROOSEVELT 1933-1945

ELEANOR ROOSEVELT
THE FIRST LADY OF THE WORLD

FALA

RECOGNITION
19 OF THE 33
USSR

THE ALPHABET AGENCIES

NATIONAL RECOVERY ADMINISTRATION

32

NRA

TVA
NLRB
WPA
CCC
SEC
SSA
OPA

FRANCES PERKINS
FIRST WOMAN CABINET MEMBER
SECRETARY OF LABOR 1933

PROHIBITION REPEALED
TWENTY-FIRST AMENDMENT
19 33

JESSE OWENS
1936
4 OLYMPIC GOLD MEDALS

FIRST TERM   MAR. 1933–JAN. 1937   SECOND TERM   JAN. 1937–JAN. 1941
THE GREAT DEPRESSION   THE NEW DEAL   LEND-LEASE   SELECTIVE SERVICE ACT

Thirty-two, Roosevelt, Franklin D.,
Four times thirty-two was he.

RELIEF · RECOVERY · WORLD WAR II

FREEDOM OF WORSHIP

FREEDOM OF SPEECH

FREEDOM FROM WANT

FREEDOM FROM FEAR

THE FOUR FREEDOMS

ALBERT EINSTEIN

$x = \frac{v}{...}$
$y = y$
$t = ...$

ENCOURAGED DEVELOPMENT OF THE ATOMIC BOMB 1939

THE UNITED NATIONS
DECLARATION

THE YALTA CONFERENCE FEBRUARY 1945

WINSTON CHURCHILL   FRANKLIN ROOSEVELT   JOSEPH STALIN

"I come from the with a firm belief a good start world   Crimea Conference that we have made on the road to peace."

JAPAN ATTACKS PEARL HARBOR DECEMBER 7, 1941

THE GLOBAL WAR

GERMANY AND ITALY DECLARE WAR ON THE UNITED   STATES DEC. 11, 1941.

MBS   BLUE   NBC   CBS

THIRD TERM   JAN. 1941 – JAN. 1945   FOURTH TERM   JAN. 1945 – APR. 1945
THE ATLANTIC CHARTER · VICTORY IN EUROPE · GERMAN REPARATIONS · UNFINISHED BUSINESS

His terms go on interminably,
"That man in the White House"—Franklin D.

Truman, Truman, Thirty-three,
Radiated energy.

Eisenhower, Thirty-four,
Inconcluded one more war.

JOHN F. KENNEDY

35

1961-1963

"Ask not what your country can do for you — ask what you can do for your country..?"

1962 CUBAN BLOCKADE

TEST BAN TREATY

1961 THE PEACE CORPS

THE BAY OF PIGS
CUBAN EXILES ARMED BY U.S. FAIL TO OVER-THROW CASTRO REGIME IN CUBA 1961

"A WORLD OF LAW AND FREE CHOICE BANISHING THE WORLD OF WAR AND COERCION."

200,000 AMERICANS IN CIVIL RIGHTS MARCH

1962 JOHN GLENN ORBITS THE EARTH

1961 FIRST ASTRONAUT ALAN SHEPARD

NOVEMBER 22,1963
JFK IS KILLED BY SNIPER AS HE RIDES IN CAR IN DALLAS

VICE PRESIDENT JOHNSON SWORN IN ON PLANE

AT 12:30 FRIDAY THE UNITED STATES PRESIDENT

Thirty-five, Kennedy, young John F.,
One more President shot to death.

LYNDON B. JOHNSON 36

The Great Society
1963-1969

"Where the meaning of man's life matches the marvels of his labor" Urban renewal Beautification Conservation
"a comfortable, useful life and an old age without worry"…
Medicare Food stamps Crime control
Antipoverty legislation
"Come now, let us reason together…"
Ghetto riots
One-half million troops in Vietnam

MEMPHIS, TENNESSEE

Free at la...
Free at l...
Thank...
Alm...
I'm...
Th...

MARTIN LUTHER KING SHOT
APRIL 4, 1968

LOS ANGELES, CA. JUNE 5, 1968
ROBERT KENNEDY SHOT TO DEATH!

"Senator Kennedy has been shot! Senator Kennedy has been shot!" Mrs. Kennedy cradled her husband's head and pleaded with the

Lyndon Johnson, Thirty-six,
More war, more death, more politics.

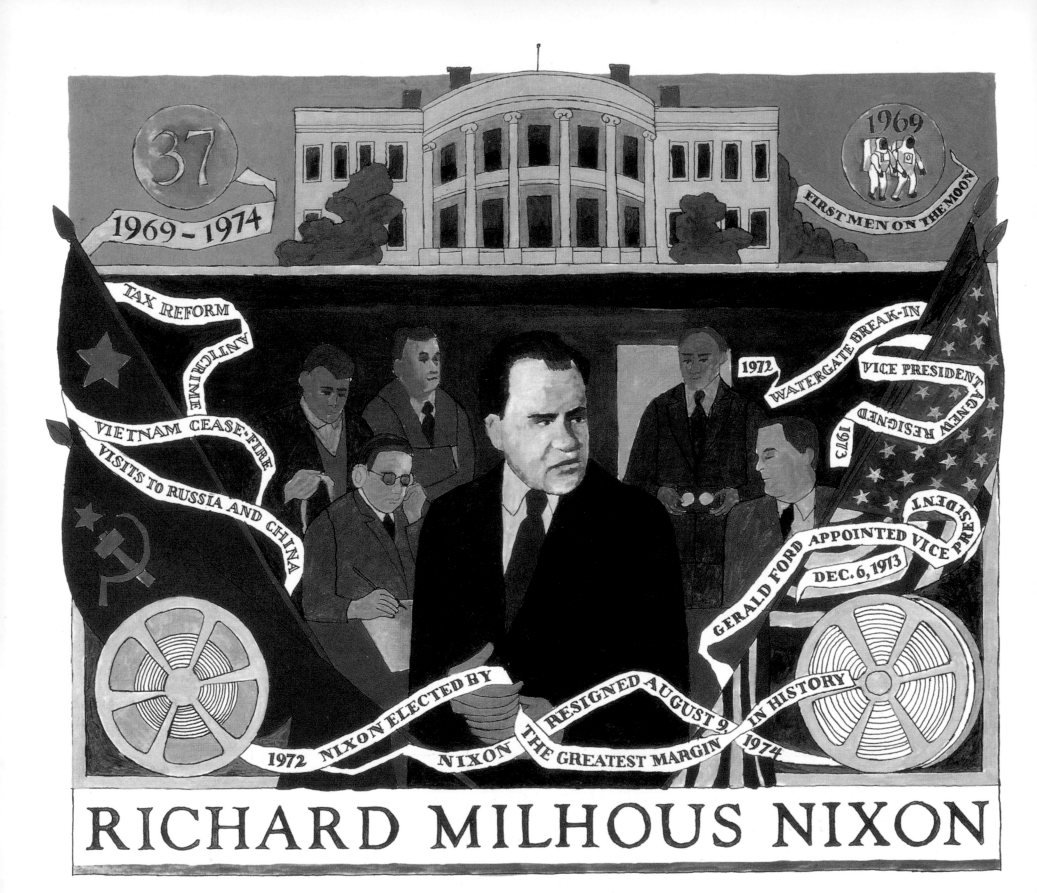

Here's Thirty-seven! Nixon, R.,
California's tarnished star.

Gerald Ford, *as Thirty-eight,*
Turned down the sound on Watergate.

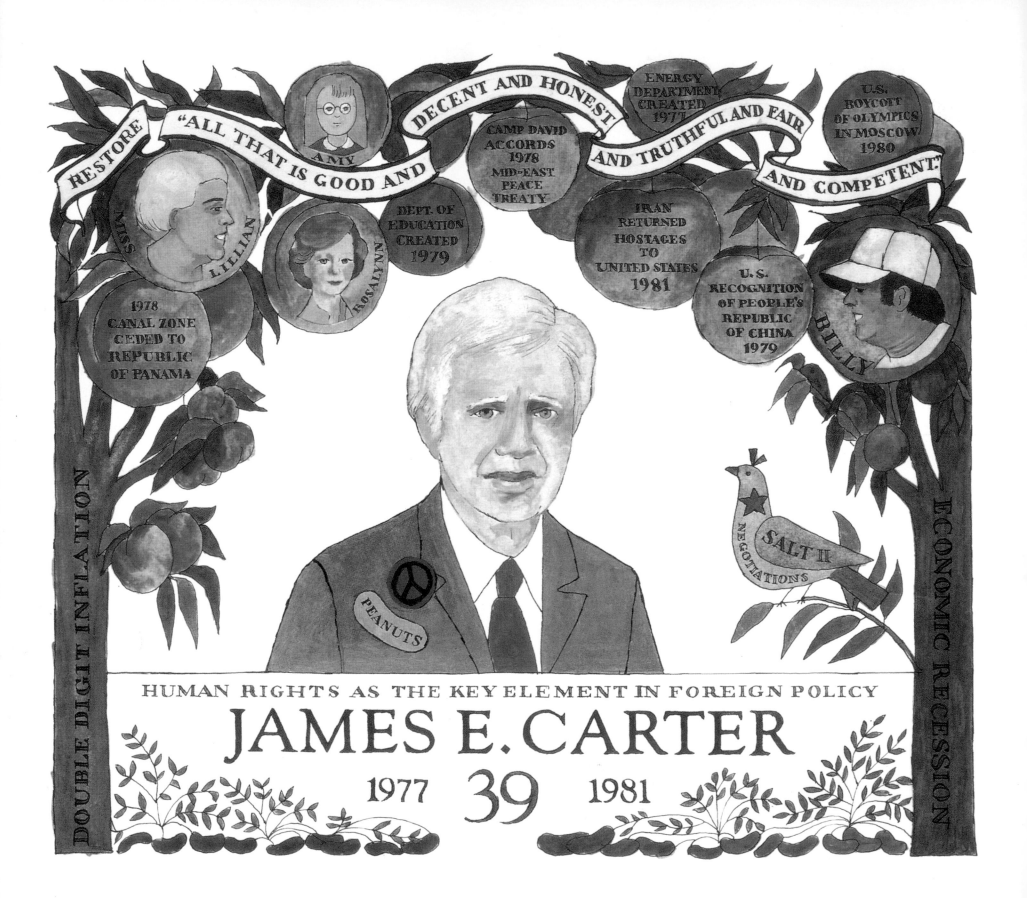

Modest Carter, Thirty-nine,
Crossed the Mason-Dixon line.

Reagan, Forty, reached his goal,
Acting out his favorite role.

Forty-one, Bush, was no one's fool:
In a troubled world, he kept his cool.

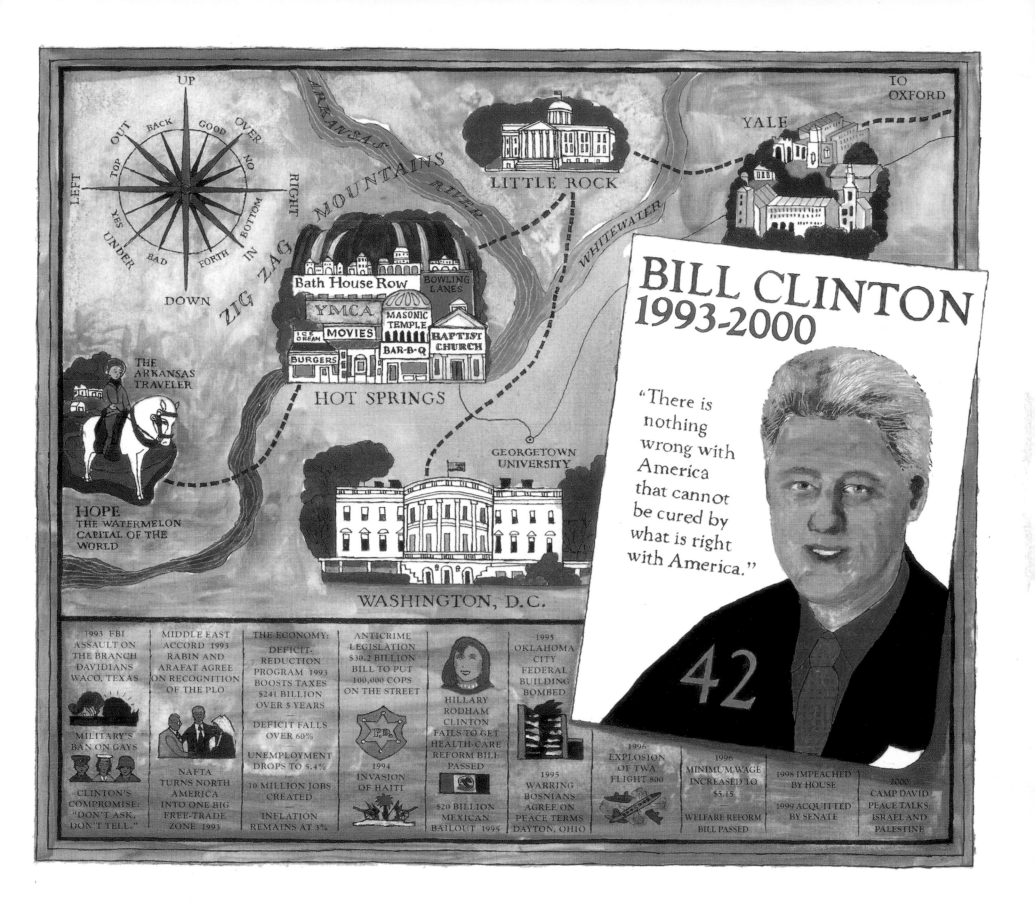

Forty-two, Clinton, quick to please,
Veered left and right and back with ease.

Junior Bush, Forty-three,
Plagued by catastrophe.

Barack Obama, Forty-four,
Cultivated hope in time of war.

NOTES ABOUT THE PRESIDENTS

1 GEORGE WASHINGTON

1789-1797   Born: February 22, 1732
Federalist   Died: December 14, 1799

The drawing is an adaptation of the Great Seal of the United States, which appears on our one-dollar bill. The Latin phrase *Annuit Coeptis*, shown next to the eye of God at the peak of the pyramid, means "He smiles upon our undertaking" or "He approves of good beginnings." The phrase occurs in *The Georgics*—a book of poems promoting agriculture—written by the poet Virgil (70–19 B.C.).

Novus Ordo Seclorum is also Latin and means "a new order of the ages." It is from Virgil's *Eclogues*—a book of pastoral idylls prophesying a world of peace where, among other things, sheep grow colored wool.

Symbolic of the diversity of the United States and its fusion under the Constitution, *E Pluribus Unum* is from Virgil's *Moretum*, wherein Virgil describes a peasant who adds one more ingredient to a very successful salad.

The seal, designed by Charles Thomson, secretary of the Continental Congress and the Constitutional Convention, reflects the agrarian interests of our American forefathers. Washington, who wanted to promote sound agronomy (the science of farming), used Virgil's *Georgics* as a starting point to warn farmers against mismanagement of their land and to inspire them to sound practices. (Source: Richard M. Gummere Jr., contributing editor, *Columbia Magazine*)

The first coin struck by the new U.S. Mint in Philadelphia was the "half-disme" (July 1792). Washington supplied some of his own silverware for the first 1,500 coins.

Washington served two terms as president. Though he didn't object to a third term on principle and could easily have won another election, he had no desire to run, thus setting a precedent that was not changed until Franklin Roosevelt took office 136 years later. Washington retired to his home at Mount Vernon, Virginia. He died less than three years after withdrawing from public life.

2 JOHN ADAMS

1797–1801   Born: October 30, 1735
Federalist   Died: July 4, 1826

Adams was the first president to occupy the Executive Mansion, designed by the French architect P. C. L'Enfant. Only six rooms were finished when he and his wife, Abigail, moved in (1800). Washington City was a small town; the entire District of Columbia contained only 3,200 people.

The war between England and France was in full swing when Adams became president. It caused difficulties for the United States on the high seas and divided the nation into partisan factions. Adams, having already helped to negotiate a treaty of peace between France and Holland, focused the attention of his administration on the French government, which had refused to negotiate with Adams's three envoys unless they would pay a substantial bribe. In

his correspondence to the Senate relating the insult, Adams referred to the Frenchman only as "X, Y, and Z." The "XYZ Affair" led to a limited and undeclared war between the United States and France (1798–1800). The successes of the new American navy gave Talleyrand, the French foreign minister, a new respect for American diplomacy. In 1800 Napoleon Bonaparte received Adams's second three-man commission; new treaties were negotiated and the "war" came to an honorable end.

3 THOMAS JEFFERSON

1801–1809   Born: April 13, 1743
Democrat-Republican   Died: July 4, 1826

Jefferson, the author of the Declaration of Independence, one of the most important documents in American history, was a remarkable man. He was a successful lawyer, architect, musician, and inventor. He spoke six languages. He was admired as a writer and thinker, and devoted himself to public service. He was a master of geopolitics.

Although the Constitution had made no provisions for the acquisition of land by the United States, Jefferson put aside any misgivings he might have had about the constitutionality of the Louisiana Purchase, which doubled the size of the country. At three cents per acre, it was surely the greatest real-estate bargain in history.

The pasha of Tripoli declared war on the United States—for refusing to pay extortion money to sail in the Mediterranean—by having the flagpole of the American consulate chopped down, Jefferson, as president, bypassed the Constitution again and declared that he had the right to defend the United States without a declaration of war by Congress. In 1805 the pasha exacted a ransom of $60,000 by threatening to kill captive Americans and forced a peace agreement—not exactly a victory for the United States. The fleet was brought home in 1807 because of the growing crisis with Great Britain. The Barbary pirates continued to prosper.

Jefferson's long correspondence with John Adams ended when they both died on the Fourth of July.

Pike discovered the peak that bears his name but failed in his attempt to climb it.

4 JAMES MADISON

1809–1817   Born: March 16, 1751
Democrat-Republican   Died: June 28, 1836

During Madison's administration, the French and British were again at war. The American policy of neutrality and peace was again compromised, and the United States found itself involved, for a second time, in a European struggle (1812). America had developed a profitable trade with both belligerents, but caught between France's and Britain's pronunciamentos, the U.S. fleet was left open to attack, its sailors to impressment.

Maintaining that by inciting Indians on the frontier, impressing sailors, and interfering with shipping, Britain was *already* at war with the United States, Madison recommended that Congress declare war.

At one point in the War of 1812, during a surprise raid on Washington, the British marines set fire to the Executive Mansion. White paint was used to cover the fire-blackened exterior, and it was thereafter known as the White House.

After two years of defeats and victories, indecisive warfare, and inconclusive invasions, a peace treaty was signed on December 24, 1814. Because of a delay in communications, America's glorious victory in New Orleans, January 8, 1815, was won after the war was officially over.

The War of 1812 was, at best, a draw. The Treaty of Ghent provided peace on the basis of an earlier status quo.

5 JAMES MONROE

1817–1825   Born: April 28, 1758
Democrat-Republican   Died: July 4, 1831

Monroe was president during a period of strengthening "nationhood" and an "era of good feelings." He was the first president to tour the country, traveling as far west as Detroit. Monroe, a bold champion of America against Europe, was greeted enthusiastically wherever he went. His policy, later known as the Monroe Doctrine, declared: "The American Continents ... are henceforth not to be considered as subjects for future colonization by any European powers."

Benjamin Lundy, an American abolitionist of Quaker origin, devoted his whole life to the antislavery cause. His weekly paper, *The Genius of Universal Emancipation*, was published irregularly until 1835.

In 1822 an abolitionist group called the American Colonization Society founded Liberia on the African coast. The society repatriated many enslaved people.

Monroe was the third president to die on the Fourth of July.

6   JOHN QUINCY ADAMS

1825–1829	Born: July 11, 1767
Democrat-Republican	Died: February 23, 1848

Eloquent John Quincy Adams was the first president who was also the son of a president. His father was John Adams, the second president of the United States.

During his term of office, John Quincy Adams arose each morning at five o'clock, built his own fire, read his Bible, and bathed in the Potomac River. One time when he was taking his morning dip, a thief ran off with his clothes. The president asked a passing boy to dash up to the White House and ask Mrs. Adams for something to wear.

Mrs. Adams, who suffered from deep depressions, preferred quiet evenings at home reading, playing her harp or composing music, and writing verse. Nevertheless, her weekly "drawing rooms" and official entertainments were always elegant and gracious occasions.

7   ANDREW JACKSON

1829–1837	Born: March 15, 1767
Democrat	Died: June 8, 1845

Unlike his predecessors, Jackson was of humble origin. He was born in a log cabin and orphaned at the age of fourteen. A child of the backwoods, he became a backwoods lawyer. Although he later became a wealthy landowner, Jacksons's appeal to his constituents lay in his common touch.

Jackson's supporters were farmers, laborers, and frontiersmen. At the president's inaugural reception, they swarmed into the White House in their boots and coonskins, trampled on the satin furniture, and overturned punch bowls, cheering him all the while. One observer called the celebration "the reign of King Mob."

Jackson warred against the chartered Bank of the United States, calling it a bank with undue economic privileges, a bank of the rich. When the time came, Jackson vetoed the bill that would recharter the bank. The American electorate approved his action.

Osceola, the famous chief of the Seminoles, put up one of the stiffest resistances to the government the Indians ever made. The United States used thousands of men and spent millions of dollars before the main strength of the Indians was broken. Those who refused to give up their freedom took refuge in the swamps of Florida. There are still bands of Seminoles who claim they have never surrendered to the United States.

8   MARTIN VAN BUREN

1837–1841	Born: December 5, 1782
Democrat	Died: July 24, 1862

Martin Van Buren was the first president born under the U.S. flag, in Kinderhook, New York. His mental ingenuity soon earned him the nickname the Red Fox.

Smiling, joking, shaking hands, Van Buren was skillful in achieving his political goals; standing five feet six inches tall, he became known as the Little Magician. He suggested the plan that ended the bank wars, which had crippled the nation's economy. Known as the Independent Treasury System, the plan was simplicity itself, but it took four years for both the House and the Senate to approve it.

Van Buren was terribly unpopular when he sought reelection in 1840, after four years of economic depression. His political opponents characterized him as "a man who drank wine from a silver goblet and ate his meals from a golden plate."

The hard times of 1837 found Samuel Morse desperate for money while working on his telegraph. When he obtained his first patent, he was financially unable to develop it. In the same year, Charles Goodyear's family was starving and Cyrus McCormick's foundry went bankrupt. Just when financial pressure drove McCormick to perfect his reaper, farmers lacked the hundred dollars needed to buy one. In 1841 McCormick finally sold two machines. (In 1851 he sold 1,000 reapers, and in 1857 23,000 were sold.)

9   WILLIAM HENRY HARRISON

1841	Born: February 9, 1773
Whig	Died: April 4, 1841

Hailed as a national hero when he led a force against the Indians at Tippecanoe Creek, in Indiana, Harrison was nicknamed Old Tippecanoe. It was here that he crushed Tecumseh, whose confederation had fought the settlers.

Harrison was sixty-eight years old at the time of his inauguration as president. Wanting to show that he was in good health, he paraded on horseback for two hours and was bareheaded when he took the Oath of Office. The day was cold and rainy. Harrison caught a cold that developed into pneumonia. He died after only thirty-two days in office.

10   JOHN TYLER

1841–1845	Born: March 29, 1790
Whig	Died: January 18, 1862

John Tyler was the first to assume the presidency on the death of his predecessor. His detractors called him His Accidency. He insisted on assuming the full powers of an elected president although he had no precedent or example to follow. He was also the first president against whom an impeachment proceeding was brought (in 1841). He was accused of misusing his veto power, but the resolution failed to pass.

Tyler had sixteen children; fifteen survived. No president has had more.

Considered to be the first clipper-type ship, the *Rainbow* was launched in January 1845. She sailed to China in ninety-two days and returned in eighty-eight. Clipper ships were to become an American symbol of beauty.

11   JAMES KNOX POLK

1845–1849	Born: November 2, 1795
Democrat	Died: June 15, 1849

Polk was committed to an expansionist policy—the nation's "Manifest Destiny." His opposition tried to take the issues of the reannexation of Texas and the reoccupation of Oregon out of the campaign, but Polk remained firm in his attitudes and even favored acquiring California at the risk of war with Mexico.

Polk, although he had been a U.S. congressman, a speaker of the house, and the governor of Tennessee, was not as well-known as his famous opponent, Senator Henry Clay. Called a "dark horse," Polk edged out Clay and became the eleventh president of the United States. (A "dark horse" is an unknown horse that may unexpectedly win a race.)

"Fifty-four forty, or fight!" was the rallying cry of extremists who sought to claim for the United State the entire Oregon territory, from the northern boundary of California to the southern boundary of Russian Alaska. Polk was willing to compromise. The British settled for the extension of the Canadian border along the forty-ninth parallel, and war between the United States and Great Britain was avoided.

12   ZACHARY TAYLOR

1849–1850	Born: November 24, 1784
Whig	Died: July 9, 1850

Taylor was the first "career" soldier to be elected to the presidency. His homespun personality was a political asset. Easy and cordial in manner, he was popular with his enlisted men, who affectionately called him Old Rough and Ready. He had no previous political training or experience and had little interest in politics prior to his election. His death (five days after attending a Fourth of July celebration) was caused by food poisoning, sunstroke, or *cholera morbus*, depending on the source of information.

Drawn more readily to personalities than to ideas, Americans embraced Taylor. He was an authentic hero.

He seemed to be a man who could settle problems. The electorate, then as now, confused great images with great behavior. Taylor's short term began a decade of failure to find an adequate leader for the United States. By 1860, when a man was nominated who *was* capable of greatness, it was too late to save the Union without bloodshed.

Whitey, Taylor's faithful old warhorse, was allowed to graze on the White House lawn.

In addition to the safety pin, Walter Hunt invented paper collars, a breech-loading rifle, an ice plow, and a pair of shoes that enabled circus clowns to walk up walls. A man of principles, Hunt never patented his version of the sewing machine. He believed that machinery that displaced people and threw them out of work was immoral.

See note under Truman with regard to "Old soldiers never die."

13 MILLARD FILLMORE

1850–1853	Born: January 7, 1800
Whig	Died: March 8, 1874

On Taylor's death, Vice President Fillmore became president. He served for three years, then failed to receive the presidential nomination in 1852. In 1856 he accepted the nomination for president by the American Party (the "Know-Nothing Party") but was defeated in the election.

Harriet Beecher Stowe's novel *Uncle Tom's Cabin* was the most telling document in the abolitionist propaganda attack. An indictment of slavery, though not of slaveholders, it sold 300,000 copies in the first year of its publication. Lincoln, on meeting Stowe, is said to have commented, "So this is the little lady who started this great big war."

In 1847 the president of the National Historical Society, Thomas Woodcock, received a crate from England containing "several pairs of small dingy birds." He released them in a city park, but none of them lived through the following winter. He repeated his experiment for several years and was rewarded with success in 1851. Sparrows now rank as major settlers in America.

In 1852 there was a prevailing prejudice that women were too stupid to be trusted alone with machines. Crowds gathered when a girl sat in a shop window to demonstrate how simple the sewing machine was to operate.

14 FRANKLIN PIERCE

1853–1857	Born: November 23, 1804
Democrat	Died: October 8, 1869

Pierce was forty-seven years old when he was elected. A true "dark horse," he was nominated at his party's convention after forty-eight ballots had eliminated all the well-known candidates.

He and his wife had three sons. The first died after only three days; the second died at the age of four. Two month before Pierce's inauguration, their third son, Benny (eleven years old), was killed in a train derailment. Benny's death put a cloud over Pierce's presidency, and Mrs. Pierce, who remained in seclusion throughout Pierce's term of office, was unable to fulfill her social obligations. The president's wife was referred to as "the ghost of the White House."

15 JAMES BUCHANAN

1857–1861	Born: April 23, 1791
Democrat	Died: June 1, 1868

James Buchanan was the only president who never married. In his youth he had been engaged to a twenty-three-year-old woman, Ann Caroline Coleman, but their engagement was broken after a quarrel. Soon after, Ann died of an overdose of laudanum, a form of opium.

Buchanan was warned by his associates that he was "sleeping on a volcano" when he refused to take a side on the controversial Dred Scott decision.

As the Southern states seceded, they confiscated U.S. property within their borders but lacked the strength to seize the offshore garrison at Fort Sumter, South Carolina. In January 1861 Buchanan ordered the unarmed merchant ship *Star of the West* to bring supplies and reinforcements to the fort. The ship was fired on by Southern shore batteries and forced to withdraw. Buchanan, with his usual indecisiveness, "reverted to a policy of inactivity that continued until he left office."

Edward M. Stanton, the president's attorney general, publicly approved of Buchanan's policies to appease the South at all costs. Privately he denounced them and was of little avail when Buchanan appealed to him for help in extricating himself from the mounting difficulties of a troubled time.

The Bonnie Blue Flag was the unofficial flag of the South (1860–1861). The flag with seven stars and three stripes became the ensign and the unofficial national flag of the Confederate States of America in March 1861.

16 ABRAHAM LINCOLN

1861–1865	Born: February 12, 1809
Republican	Died: April 15, 1865

Considered a "small-time prairie politician" by his contemporaries, Lincoln took office at a momentous time in the history of the United States. The nation was divided into two separate, hostile countries with what seemed like irreconcilable differences.

The South itself was divided. Maryland, Delaware, Kentucky, and Missouri, all Southern slave states, stayed with the Union. Forty-six mountain counties in northwest Virginia refused to accept the decision to secede and established a "loyal" government. (They were accepted into the United States as West Virginia.)

Lincoln's policy to meet the crisis was clear: Secession was illegal. No state could of its own volition leave the Union. Acts of violence to support secession were to be considered insurrectionary. The federal government would execute the laws in all the states and maintain possession of all federal property in the seceded states.

To support this policy, Lincoln dispatched a naval relief expedition to Fort Sumter. Rather than bow to federal authority and in order to sustain secession, the Confederate States fired on Fort Sumter on April 21, 1861, before the ships arrived—the first shots of the Civil War.

The war began within two months of Lincoln's taking office and ended the month he died.

On April 14, 1865, under the impression that he was helping the South, John Wilkes Booth, a crazed actor, shot Lincoln, who was attending a performance at Ford's Theatre in Washington. Shouting the state of Virginia's motto, *Sic Semper Tyrannis* ("Ever thus to tyrants"), Booth, the self-appointed avenging angel, leaped from Lincoln's box to the stage, breaking a leg in the fall. Brandishing a knife he presumably had carried in case his gun misfired, he escaped from the theater. After a frantic two-week search by the army and the Secret Service, Booth was cornered. He either shot himself or was shot by his pursuers.

A myth that Booth escaped with his life still persists.

17 ANDREW JOHNSON

1865–1869	Born: December 29, 1808
Democrat	Died: July 31, 1875

Johnson's parents had been too poor to send him to school. He was apprenticed to a tailor when he was fourteen years old but ran away to open his own tailor shop. Largely self-taught, Johnson never did attend school He was hardly able to read when he married Eliza McCardle and was about seventeen years old when she taught him to write. Nevertheless, he was an effective speaker and took part in debates at the local academy. He became even more adept as a "stump speaker" when he entered politics. He nominated himself for the Tennessee legislature and was elected. When he was nominated as Lincoln's vice president, he is said to have asked, "What will the aristocrats do?"

The Tenure of Office Act of March 2, 1867, prohibited the president from removing a cabinet member without the consent of Congress. In defiance of this act, Johnson dismissed his secretary of war. Impeachment proceedings were started by Congress on February 24, 1868. The resolution charged Johnson with "high crimes and misdemeanors, usurpation of the law, corrupt use of veto power and interference at elections." Johnson would have been impeached but for *one* vote.

18   ULYSSES SIMPSON GRANT

1869–1877	Born: April 27, 1822
Republican	Died: July 23, 1885

A West Point graduate, Grant fought under General Zachary Taylor in the Mexican War, then resigned his commission because he didn't feel he could support his wife on army pay. He rejoined the army at the advent of the Civil War. His conspicuous successes caused Lincoln to appoint him commander of all the Union armies. He led them to victory.

On the capitulation of the South, Grant permitted the Southern soldiers to keep their horses for spring plowing and wrote generous surrender terms, disallowing treason trials. He became a national hero and easily won his election to the presidency.

Unfortunately, Grant surrounded himself with corrupt politicians who cheated, stole, and took bribes. Honest himself, he innocently took expensive presents from his hangers-on. He also took the blame for emerging scandals.

Gant realized too late that speculators Jay Gould and James Fisk were trying to corner the market in gold. By the time he took action against them, the economy was already in turmoil. Grant's administration is synonymous with the poorest statesmanship and lowest moral ebb in our history.

19   RUTHERFORD BIRCHARD HAYES

1877–1881	Born: October 4, 1822
Republican	Died: January 17, 1893

Known first as His Fraudulency (he had gained the presidency by only one electoral vote, causing his election to be disputed), Hayes soon commanded respect as a firm, serious, honest, hardworking president.

He saw the end of the reconstruction of the South and encouraged its self-government. He pledged protection of "Negro rights" and insisted that his appointments were to be made based on *merit*.

In spite of both his and Mrs. Hayes's views on temperance, their entertainments at the White House were popular.

Hayes declined to run for a second term.

20   JAMES ABRAM GARFIELD

1881	Born: November 19, 1831
Republican	Died: September 19, 1881

Garfield, on the morning of Lincoln's death, cried out, "God reigns and the government in Washington still lives." One might have thought that he had foreknowledge of his own assassination.

Less than four months after taking office, Garfield was shot while waiting for a train in a Washington station. Charles Guiteau, an attorney, frustrated and melancholy at not receiving a government job, had stepped out and fired at the president. Garfield languished in pain for eighty days.

Alexander Graham Bell tried to locate the assassin's bullet, still embedded in the president's body, with an "induction balance electrical device" he had invented. He had no luck. (The X-ray was not invented until fourteen years later.) Guiteau was tried and hanged on June 30, 1882.

In many areas of the West, the mail was carried by stages or riders contracted by the Post Office Department. A star was used to designate these postal routes. Garfield's postmaster general investigated and exposed contracts that had been fraudulently awarded to unscrupulous politicians.

21   CHESTER ALAN ARTHUR

1881–1885	Born: October 5, 1830
Republican	Died: November 18, 1886

On the death of Garfield, his vice president became the nation's leader. Arthur, who had been a "machine" politician adhering to his party's every policy, reformed when he became president. He avoided his old political friends, who had expected him to hand out jobs to them. They were dismayed by the "new Arthur" when he recommended a civil service law curtailing political patronage and establishing a Civil Service Commission (1883).

Garfield's shocking assassination and Hayes's austere administration had made the White House ambience too gloomy for the newly elected Arthur. He ordered the White House redecorated. Twenty-four wagonloads of old things were hauled away to make room for his new furnishings. He himself became a man of fashion. He entertained lavishly (he had a French cook) and associated himself with the social elite of Newport (Rhode Island), Washington, and New York.

22, 24   STEPHEN GROVER CLEVELAND

1885–1889	Born: March 18, 1837
1893–1897	Died: June 24, 1908
Democrat	

Cleveland was the only president to leave the White House and return for a second term after four years' absence. (He ran again at the end of his first term but was defeated by Benjamin Harrison.)

A bachelor when he moved into the White House, Cleveland found its comforts made him uneasy. He yearned for a "pickled herring" to eat instead of "the French stuff."

Grover Cleveland was the only president to be married in the White House (June 2, 1886). Frances Folsom Cleveland gave state entertainments a new interest—working women were free to come to her Saturday-afternoon receptions. She became one of the most popular of all the nation's hostesses.

23   BENJAMIN HARRISON

1889–1893	Born: August 20, 1833
Republican	Died: March 13, 1901

Harrison, who was five feet six inches tall, was derisively called Little Ben by his opponents. His supporters replied that he was big enough to wear his "grandfather's hat," which became his nickname. (His grandfather, William Henry Harrison, "Old Tippecanoe," had been the ninth president of the United States.)

Harrison's demeanor was cold and unfriendly. He was not popular with either the people or the politicians. As an incumbent, he ran against Cleveland again in 1892, but this time Cleveland won.

25   WILLIAM McKINLEY

1897–1901	Born: January 29, 1843
Republican	Died: September 14, 1901

McKinley, one of our best-loved presidents, twice defeated the persuasive orator William Jennings Bryan in the race for the presidency. The principal issue was imperialism, and America embarked on a program of overseas expansion.

McKinley was called the "advance agent of prosperity" and advocated "the full dinner pail," which appealed to working-class voters.

McKinley was standing in a receiving line at the Pan-American Exposition in Buffalo when an anarchist, Leon Czolgosz, shouting that the president was "an enemy of good working people," shot him (September 6, 1901). McKinley died eight days later. Czolgosz was judged sane and was executed.

26 THEODORE ROOSEVELT

1901–1909
Republican
Born: October 27, 1858
Died: January 6, 1919

Succeeding to the presidency after McKinley's assassination, Roosevelt, at forty-two, became the youngest president in the nation's history—and the most colorful. He energetically committed himself to a life of strenuous endeavor. An enemy of the giant trusts, a crusader for conservation, he worked vigorously for a progressive domestic program.

Roosevelt also steered the United States into a more active involvement in world politics, quoting the proverb "Speak softly and carry a big stick. . . ."

Although he was nicknamed Four-eyes, he boxed, hunted, rode horseback, and romped with his lively children. He was the first president to ride in an automobile and the first to fly in an airplane.

He wrote books on politics, history, America, literature, and womanhood, as well as several about ranch life, outdoor pastimes, the wilderness, and great adventures and holidays in the open.

Appreciative of the joys inherent in the "great outdoors," Roosevelt added 125 million acres to our national forest system.

27 WILLIAM HOWARD TAFT

1909–1913
Republican
Born: September 15, 1857
Died: March 8, 1930

Taft was an immense man. He was six feet two inches tall and weighed more than three hundred pounds. In sprite of his bulk, he was a graceful dancer and a good tennis player. He was full of good humor and liked to have fun. He tossed out the first ball of the 1910 baseball season, a custom followed since by many presidents.

He characterized his presidential campaign as "one of the most uncomfortable four months of my life." Taft considered the White House to be "the loneliest place in the world," and when Harding, to honor him, appointed him Chief Justice of the Supreme Court, he wrote, "I don't remember that I was ever President."

28 THOMAS WOODROW WILSON

1913–1921
Democrat
Born: December 28, 1856
Died: February 3, 1924

Quiet and respected, Wilson won his election to the presidency by an overwhelming electoral vote, though not by popular majority.

Wilson was a reformer. He endorsed a program calling for a lower tariff, a graduated federal income tax, stronger antitrust laws, and a federal money system.

War in Europe broke out in 1914, and anti-German feelings ran high. Sauerkraut was renamed "liberty cabbage" and hamburger became "liberty sausage." German music was banned in some areas, as was the teaching of German in some public schools. The Los Angeles Public Library dumped all of its German books. The Espionage Act (June 1917), Sabotage Act (April 1918), and the Sedition Act (May 1918) were passed.

In 1917, when German submarines sank U.S. ships, America could no longer remain neutral, and Wilson asked Congress for a declaration of war on Germany. He called it "a war to end war," and even before it was over he presented Congress with his proposal for a League of Nations. Wilson was bitterly disappointed when the Senate voted it down.

Eugene V. Debs, organizer of the American Railway Union, ran for president five times on the Socialist Party ticket. An honest, idealistic labor leader, Debs was not pro-German, but he *was* a pacifist. He was arrested and tried under the Espionage Act of 1917 and sentenced to ten years in a federal penitentiary in the fall of 1918. The Supreme Court upheld his conviction in 1919. Debs was in the Atlantic Penitentiary the last time he ran for office—receiving 919,799 votes (1920).

29 WARREN GAMALIEL HARDING

1921–1923
Republican
Born: November 2, 1865
Died: August 2, 1923

"Harding looked like a president," said one of his admirers (Harry Daugherty). It was his main qualification for being one.

Harding's unscrupulous appointees began using their political posts for their own financial benefit. He allowed political party bosses to determine his policies. They easily obtained the president's signature on their bills.

Harding's administration was rife with scandals and the theft of government funds. One of his cabinet members went to jail for taking bribes.

Dismayed and out of control, Harding traveled as far as California trying to present his side of the story to the people. He died of a heart attack before indictments in the biggest scandal of all, Teapot Dome, were handed down.

30 JOHN CALVIN COOLIDGE

1923–1929
Republican
Born: July 4, 1872
Died: January 5, 1933

Walter Lippmann suggested in 1926 that Coolidge's political genius "was a talent for effectively doing nothing." The president's passivity suited businessmen who wanted to be left alone. They needn't have worried; Coolidge was on their side anyway.

His philosophy was: "The man who builds a factory, builds a temple. The man who works there, worships there."

He stood for economy, tax cuts, isolationism, and limited aid to farmers. He did nothing to check the uneasy economic boom.

Coolidge was surprisingly witty, considering his taciturnity. When a woman told him she had made a bet that she could get him to say more than two words, he looked her straight in the eye and said, "You lose."

Two anarchists, Nicola Sacco and Bartolomeo Vanzetti, were tried, found guilty, and executed for the robbery and murder of a payroll guard.

The trial, coming as it did so shortly after the war aged by Attorney General A. Mitchell Palmer against both labor unions and radicals, made civil liberties advocates believe that Sacco and Vanzetti were being tried for being anarchists rather than on a sound basis on criminal evidence. The case became the cause célèbre of the 1920s.

Sacco and Vanzetti were executed in August 1927.

31 HERBERT CLARK HOOVER

1929–1933
Republican
Born: August 10, 1874
Died: October 20, 1964

In 1928, when he was nominated for president, Hoover said, "We in America are nearer to the final triumph over poverty than ever before in the history of any land."

In reality, prosperity was at an end for farmers and nearly so for business. On October 21, 1929, stocks were down, and five days later the stock market collapsed. The causes of the crash and the financial panic that followed were debated for years afterward.

Hoover tried to develop a program to combat the Great Depression, but the economy continued to sink lower. He abandoned his notion that volunteers could save the situation, but his cautious attempts at government action were ineffective. The nation was in despair.

In the summer of 1932, veterans of World War I marched on Washington and demanded, to no avail, immediate payment of a bonus for their services in the war. Half of them accepted Hoover's offer of a fare home. He ordered the army to evict the remainder. The evicting soldiers, under the command of Chief of Staff Douglas MacArthur, with his aides Dwight D. Eisenhower and George Patton, who were themselves to become famous veterans, drove out the bonus marchers and burned their encampment.

32 FRANKLIN DELANO ROOSEVELT

1933–1945   Born: January 30, 1882
Democrat   Died: April 12, 1945

Stricken with poliomyelitis when he was thirty-nine years old, Roosevelt, with great courage and an indomitable spirit, fought to retain the use of his legs. He learned to move using heavy braces, crutches, and a wheelchair. His favorite hobby, stamp collecting, must have seen him through many difficult periods.

He brought the same spirit to the White House. Promising the country a "New Deal," Roosevelt tackled the Great Depression with zest. In his first one hundred days in office, an innovative program was exacted to bring recovery to the desperate nation. This bold National Recovery Administration (NRA) challenged the government to act in every aspect of the nation's economy and culture with these and other so-called "Alphabet Agencies":

TVA	Tennessee Valley Authority
NLRB	National Labor Relations Board
WPA	Works Progress Administration
CCC	Civilian Conservation Corps
SEC	Securities and Exchange Commission
SSA	Social Security Administration
OPA	Office of Price Administration

The American people approved. They elected Roosevelt again. And again. And again.

His opponents were dismayed. "That man in the White House" was going to remain there forever, it seemed.

Roosevelt died April 12, 1945, less than a month before World War II ended in Europe. No other president served as long as Roosevelt, and no other will. The Twenty-second Amendment (ratified in 1951) states: "No person shall be elected to the Office of President more than twice."

FDR was the first president to use mass media extensively. His famous Fireside Chats were broadcast over all the major radio networks of the time. He was also the first president to appear on television (April 30, 1939).

FDR was a distant cousin to Theodore Roosevelt.

33 HARRY S. TRUMAN

1945–1953   Born: May 8, 1884
Democrat   Died: December 26, 1972

The Germans surrendered unconditionally to Allied forces on May 7, 1945. Truman, then president, saw the end of the war with Japan. His most difficult decision was whether or not to use the atomic bomb.

He kept a sign on his desk to remind himself that when the responsibility for making a decision reaches the president, he must make that decision alone. It read: the buck stops here. The president can ask for advice, but he has to make up his mind by himself. His choices sometimes require vision and courage, for they can commit a whole nation to a course that will have permanent and vital effects on history. Truman wrote in his memoirs: "To be President of the United States is to be lonely, very lonely at times of great decisions."

General Douglas MacArthur, commander of the U.S. Army in Asia, disagreed sharply with Truman's policy of *limited* involvement in the Korean War. He made his views on the matter public, concluding, "There is no substitute for victory," in the hope of reversing administration policies. Truman relieved him of his command on April 11, 1951. MacArthur was quoting from an old barracks ballad when he said that "old soldiers never die; they just fade away" in his farewell address to Congress.

34 DWIGHT DAVID EISENHOWER

1953–1961   Born: October 14, 1890
Republican   Died: March 28, 1969

Eisenhower (nicknamed Ike) became president when the undeclared Korean War was at full tilt. Ike helped negotiate its end. Officially only a "police action," the war had lasted more than three years and cost the United States 25,000 dead, more than 115,000 other casualties, and $22 billion. In 1953 the signing of a truce brought an indefinite and uneasy peace along the border between North and South Korea. For those who liked to think in terms of total victory, such a truce seemed painfully inconclusive.

Eisenhower's term of office is known as the businessman's administration. Charles E. Wilson, at the hearing for his appointment as Ike's secretary of defense, said he assumed that "what is good for the country is good for General Motors" and vice versa.

It was Adlai Stevenson (Ike's opponent in the 1952 and 1956 elections) who commented, "the New Dealers have all left Washington to make way for the car dealers."

The little *Vanguard I*, a test satellite nicknamed Grapefruit, was put into orbit in 1958. It weighed only 3-1/4 pounds and transmitted for years.

35 JOHN FITZGERALD KENNEDY

1961–1963   Born: May 29, 1917
Democrat   Died: November 22, 1963

Kennedy was the youngest person to be elected president and the youngest to die in office. He was killed while driving through Dallas in a motorcade. In the open car were his wife, Jacqueline, and Texas governor John B. Connally and his wife, Nellie.

Shots from a long-range rifle killed Kennedy and wounded Connally. Kennedy was assassinated by Lee Harvey Oswald, a deranged Cuban sympathizer. Taken into custody after his arrest, Oswald was himself shot to death two days later by nightclub owner Jack Ruby. Ruby was charged with murder and jailed.

The Warren Commission, which investigated the death of Kennedy, concluded that Oswald was acting as an individual and that there was no conspiracy involved. However, many unanswered questions about the president's death remain.

36 LYNDON BAINES JOHNSON

1963–1969   Born: August 27, 1908
Democrat   Died: January 22, 1973

Johnson, who had followed Kennedy to Dallas in *Air Force Two* (presidents and vice presidents never fly together for national security reasons), flew back to Washington, D.C., in *Air Force One*. He was sworn in as chief executive in the course of the trip.

The first thing he did as president was to help enact Kennedy's new civil rights bill. When he ran for election in 1964, Johnson was elected by a popular margin of fifteen million votes.

He himself proposed and pushed through many programs for social and economic reform, but he was unlucky. Unrest and rioting persisted in the inner-city ghettos in spite of antipoverty and antidiscrimination programs, and the controversy over the war in Vietnam escalated.

Johnson withdrew as a candidate for reelection in order to seek, unhampered by political considerations, solutions to the nation's problems.

37 RICHARD MILHOUS NIXON

1969–1974   Born: January 9, 1913
Republican   Died: April 22, 1994

Nixon was the first president to resign from the office.

Police had arrested five men who had broken into and installed wiretapping devices in Democratic headquarters in the Watergate office building before the election in 1972. Nixon and his associates tried to conceal their own involvement in this crime. Much incriminating evidence was discovered on the White House tape recorders.

The Senate, after exhaustive investigation, recommended impeachment proceedings. Nixon resigned in disgrace on

August 9, 1974. Seven of his former aides were indicted in the Watergate conspiracy.

Nixon's vice president, Spiro T. Agnew, had reigned in 1973 as a result of unrelated scandals. Nixon subsequently chose Gerald R. Ford as his vice president.

Neil Armstrong (commander of the *Apollo 11* mission) and Edwin Aldrin were the first men to set foot on the moon, on July 20, 1969.

38 GERALD RUDOLF FORD
1974–1977   Born: July 14, 1913
Republican   Died: December 26, 2006

Ford succeeded to the presidency when Nixon resigned. As he had been *appointed* vice president, he became our only unelected president. He, by his patent honesty, did much to unify the country.

Ford did his best to curb mounting inflation and stimulate the economy. He won the nomination for president in 1976 but the shadow of Watergate clung to him. He was defeated by Jimmy Carter

39 JAMES EARL CARTER
1977–1981   Born: October 1, 1924
Democrat   Died:

Prior to Jimmy Carter's election, the president's often embarrassing brother, Billy, said, "My mother joined the Peace Corps when she was seventy, my sister Gloria is a motorcycle racer, my other sister, Ruth, is a Holy Roller preacher, and my brother thinks he's going to be president of the United States! I'm really the only normal one in my family."

Carter was the first president from the Deep South in more than a century. An unpretentious man, he spoke of himself as a "simple country boy," which hardly describes an Annapolis graduate, an experienced naval officer, a student of nuclear physics, a state senator, and then a governor of Georgia.

His administration was plagued by the first "hostage crisis." After fourteen months of difficult negotiations, the hostages held captive by Iran were finally released on the same day that Carter left office.

Protesting the Soviet invasion of Afghanistan, Carter ordered a U.S. boycott of the Olympic Games in Moscow in 1980.

40 RONALD WILSON REAGAN
1981–1989   Born: February 6, 1911
Republican   Died: June 5, 2004

Reagan was the only professional actor to become president. He had appeared in more than fifty movies, had been host on two dramatic TV shows, and had been president of the Screen Actors Guild. He had also been governor of California.

He referred to himself as the Gipper, a nickname from one of his movie roles, and published (with a collaborator) an autobiography titled *Where's the Rest of Me?* (a line from one of his films).

Reagan's effective use of TV in presenting his administration's programs earned him the nickname of the Great Communicator.

Ronald Reagan initiated legislation to curb inflation, improve economic growth, and strengthen the possibility of full employment. He improved U.S. relations with the Soviet Union and spoke out strongly against terrorism. Unfortunately, Reagan's administration was beset by scandals: waste and fraud in the Department of Housing and Urban Development; environmental violations at the government's nuclear weapons plants; greed in the bankrupt Savings and Loan Association; and finally, the Iran-Contra Affair.

41 GEORGE HERBERT WALKER BUSH
1989–1993   Born: June 12, 1924
Republican   Died:

During George Bush's four-year term as president, no single action received more attention or derision than when he reneged on his central campaign pledge: "Read my lips: No new taxes." Soon after taking office, Bush sanctioned various tax hikes and higher Medicare premiums. In 1992 he apologized to the American people for these tax increases.

Following in the footsteps of his predecessors, Bush continued to increase aid to the regime of Saddam Hussein, allegedly hoping to woo Iraq into "the family of nations." Hussein garnered more than five billion dollars in load guarantees from the Reagan and Bush administrations, and as a result, Iraq became a major military power. Bush's foreign-aid policy backfired when Iraq invaded and occupied oil-rich Kuwait in 1990. Under the aegis of the United Nations and with a clear mandate from Congress, Bush ordered an all-out military attack on Iraq. Kuwait was liberated within thirty days. The swift victory of the United States raised Bush's approval rating to 89 percent. Saddam Hussein, despite his humiliating defeat, managed to survive President Bush in power.

The major emphasis of U.S. foreign policy since World War II had been to counter the threat of the Soviet Union and the expansion of Communism. Bush was president during a period of startling changes in Eastern Europe: Communism seemed to collapse under its own weight and the Berlin wall fell.

In Bush's words, "By the Grace of God, America won the Cold War." However, Bush failed to explain or interpret

these momentous events or point out the challenges and opportunities or the dangers occasioned by the dismantling of the Soviets.

42 WILLIAM JEFFERSON CLINTON
1993–2001   Born: August 19, 1946
Democrat   Died:

In 1992 Dick Morris, who at the time was a political adviser to President Clinton, observed: "Bill Clinton has a very true compass. . . . But within the general proposition he wants to go north, he will take an endless variety of routes. He's constantly maneuvering, constantly picking the routes he wants to get there, maneuvering his opponents into positions where they can't get a clear shot at him."

If *north* can be taken to mean the White House, then it can be said he started on his travels while still in high school. In 1963 he attended a national convention of Boys' Nation (an American Legion-affiliated leadership organization), during which he was photographed with President John F. Kennedy. It was then that Bill Clinton decided to become a politician instead of a musician, a teacher, or a minister, options he had considered. The picture taken with JFK is said to be Clinton's most cherished possession.

After completing his education, Clinton settled down to practice law in Little Rock, Arkansas. He entered politics and at the age of 32 was elected governor of the state, which put him well on his way *north*.

Bill Clinton was sworn in as the forty-second president of the United States on January 20, 1993.

The first two years of his administration were plagued by controversial political appointments, Congressional inquiries into the Whitewater real estate imbroglio, and alleged personal improprieties. These, along with the failure of his ambitious health-care reform plan, threatened to eclipse the genuine advances he made in world trade while strengthening the economy, education, and anti-crime legislation in the United States. "Character" questions continued to dog Clinton into his second term, culminating in his impeachment by the House and subsequent acquittal by the Senate on charges of obstruction of justice.

43 GEORGE W. BUSH
2001–2009   Born: July 6, 1946
Republican   Died:

George W. Bush took office early in 2001, following one of the most controversial presidential races in United States history—a race in which opponent Al Gore actually won the popular vote but lost in the electoral college after a dispute over ballots in Florida, subsequent recounts, and a Supreme Court decision.

Tragedy struck soon after with the September 11, 2001, attacks on the United States. That morning, nineteen al Qaeda terrorists hijacked four commercial passenger airplanes. They intentionally crashed three of them into the two World Trade Center towers in New York City and the Pentagon outside Washington, D.C. After resistance from passengers and crew, the fourth crashed in a field near Shanksville, Pennsylvania. Bush subsequently declared a global War on Terrorism and ordered the invasion of Afghanistan to overthrow the Taliban, destroy al Qaeda, and capture al Qaeda leader Osama bin Laden. Less than a year and a half later, in 2003, Bush ordered the invasion of Iraq, launching the Iraq War against Saddam Hussein and the Ba'ath Party government. Both of these conflicts would last into his successor's presidency.

Tragedy reared its head again early in Bush's second term when an epic storm began brewing over the Bahamas. Hurricane Katrina made landfall in the southeast United States, leaving horrific scenes of devastation in its wake. At least 1,830 people lost their lives, making Katrina one of the deadliest hurricanes in U.S. history, and the most expensive as well—there was a staggering $81 billion worth of damages.

mering out a bill to overhaul the health care system and fending off attacks from a new populist protest movement called the Tea Party. Reactions to global warming took on more urgency; nevertheless, many individuals continued to deny that a problem even existed. An era of great technological advance was also underway, with the advent of electronic readers, hybrid cars, and the rise of solar power applications.

Obama appointed his former rival for the presidential nomination, Senator (and former first lady) Hillary Rodham Clinton, as Secretary of State. Another notable appointment was Sonia Sotomayor, the first Hispanic Supreme Court justice.

As much an icon as the president himself, Obama's wife, Michelle, rose to popularity as the first lady, setting out to combat childhood obesity and planting a vegetable garden on the White House lawn with her two daughters and local schoolchildren to promote sustainability and healthy living.

44   BARACK HUSSEIN OBAMA

2009–   Born: August 4, 1961
Democrat   Died:

From the outset, Barack Obama built his campaign for presidency around the prospect of change, and change was indeed afoot in the United States when he took office in 2009 as the country's first African American president. Born in Honolulu, Hawaii, Obama was also the first president born outside the continental United States.

Among other problems, Obama inherited the greatest financial crisis since the Great Depression of 1929. Millions of Americans had lost their jobs and homes, and the stock market had plummeted, during the near-collapse of the U.S. banking system in the fall of 2008. In February 2009, Obama signed into law the American Recovery and Reinvestment Act, a $1.1 trillion federal stimulus plan that made major investments in such things as clean energy, health care, and education. The economy began to show signs of recovery as 2009 turned into 2010.

Obama spent a good part of his first year in office ham-

SELECTED BIBLIOGRAPHY

Bridgewater, William, and Seymour Kurtz, editors. *The Columbia Encyclopedia*, 3rd ed. New York and London: Columbia University Press, 1963.

Catton, Bruce, and Oliver Jensen, editors. *American Heritage: The Magazine of History*. New York: American Heritage Publishing Co. Issues December 1956 through August 1964.

Current, Richard N., T. Harry Williams, and Frank Freidel. *American History: A Survey*. New York: Alfred A. Knopf, 1961.

David, Donald, author of the text and general editor. *Divided We Fought: A Pictorial History of the War, 1861–1865*. New York: The Macmillan Company, 1952.

DeGregorio, William A. *The Complete Book of U.S. Presidents*, 4th ed. New York: Wings Books, 1993.

Dunbar, Seymour. *A History of Travel in America*. New York: Tudor Publishing Company, 1937.

Freidel, Frank. *The Presidents of the United States of America*, 11th ed. Washington: White House Historical Association with the cooperation of the National Geographic Society, 1987.

Hanser, Richard, and Donald B. Hyatt. *Meet Mr. Lincoln*. New York: A Ridge Press Book/Golden Press, 1960.

Kane, John Nathan. *Facts about the Presidents*. New York: The H. W. Wilson Company, 1959.

Klapthor, Margaret Brown. *The First Ladies*, 5th ed. Washington: White House Historical Association with the cooperation of the National Geographic Association, 1987.

LaFarge, Oliver. *A Pictorial History of the American Indian*. New York: Crown Publishers, Inc., 1956.

Lorant, Stefan. *FDR: A Pictorial Biography*. New York: Simon & Schuster, 1950.

Pett, Saul, Sid Moody, Hugh Mulligan, and Tom Henshaw. *The Torch Is Passed: The Associated Press Story of the Death of a President*. New York: The Associated Press, 1963.

Schmitt, Martin F., and Dee Brown. *Fighting Indians of the West*. New York: Charles Scribner's Sons, 1948.

Smith, Whitney. *The Flag Book of the United States*. New York: William Morrow and Company, 1970.

Sullivan, George. *Mr. President: A Book of U.S. Presidents*. New York: Scholastic Inc., 1984.

Taylor, John W. R., and Kenneth Munson. *History of Aviation*. New York: Crown Publishers, reprinted 1972.

Wilson, Mitchell. *American Science and Invention: A Pictorial History*. New York: Simon & Schuster, 1954.